PlayTime® Piano

Favorites

Level 1

5-Finger Melodies

This book belongs to: **Srisha.V**

Arranged by

Nancy and Randall Faber

Production: Frank and Gail Hackinson
Production Coordinator: Marilyn Cole
Cover: Terpstra Design, San Francisco
Music Editor: Edwin McLean
Engraving: Tempo Music Press, Inc.

FABER
PIANO ADVENTURES®
3042 Creek Drive
Ann Arbor, Michigan 48108

A NOTE TO TEACHERS

PlayTime® Piano Favorites is a carefully chosen collection of well-known folk songs and children's favorites. The pieces are useful for recital performances, family or group sing-alongs, and as motivational material for private or group lessons.

The songs are arranged in Middle C Position and C Position (5-finger scale in C). These familiar songs are excellent for reinforcing note names and interval recognition.

PlayTime® Piano Favorites is part of the *PlayTime® Piano* series arranged by Faber and Faber. "PlayTime" designates Level 1 of the *PreTime® to BigTime® Piano Supplementary Library,* and it is available in a variety of styles including Popular, Classics, Rock 'n Roll, Jazz & Blues, Christmas and Hymns.

Following are the levels of the supplementary library, which lead from *PreTime®* to *BigTime®.*

PreTime® Piano	(Primer Level)
PlayTime® Piano	(Level 1)
ShowTime® Piano	(Level 2A)
ChordTime® Piano	(Level 2B)
FunTime® Piano	(Level 3A – 3B)
BigTime® Piano	(Level 4)

Each level offers books in a variety of styles, making it possible for the teacher to offer stimulating material for every student. For a complimentary detailed listing email faber@pianoadventures.com or write us at the mailing address below.

Visit **pianoadventures.com**.

Teacher Duets

Optional teacher duets are a valuable feature of the *PlayTime® Piano* series. Although the arrangements stand complete on their own, the duets provide a fullness of harmony and rhythmic vitality. And not incidentally, they offer the opportunity for parent and student to play together.

Helpful Hints:

1. The student should know his or her part thoroughly before the teacher duet is used. Accurate rhythm is especially important.

2. Rehearsal numbers are provided to give the student and teacher starting places.

3. The teacher may wish to count softly a measure before beginning, as this will help the ensemble.

ISBN 978-1-61677-013-6

TABLE OF CONTENTS

4

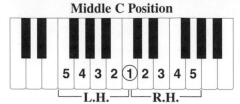

Middle C Position

L.H. — 5 4 3 2 ① R.H. — 1 2 3 4 5

① —thumbs share Middle C

Down in the Valley

Not too fast

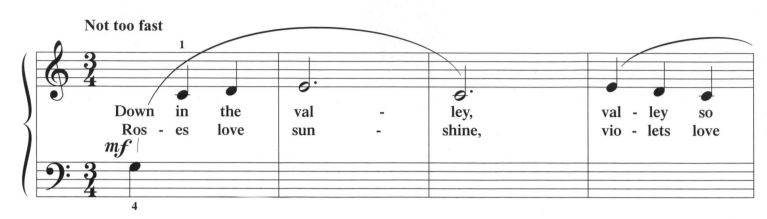

Down in the val - ley,   val - ley so
Ros - es love sun - shine,   vio - lets love

mf

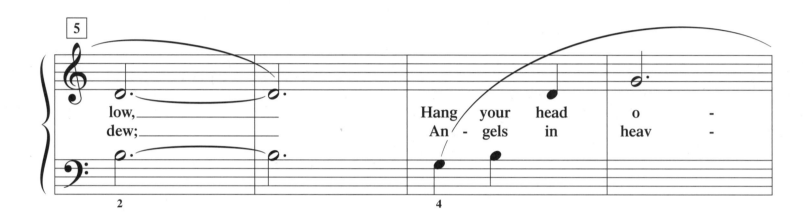

low,_____   Hang your head o -
dew;_____   An - gels in heav -

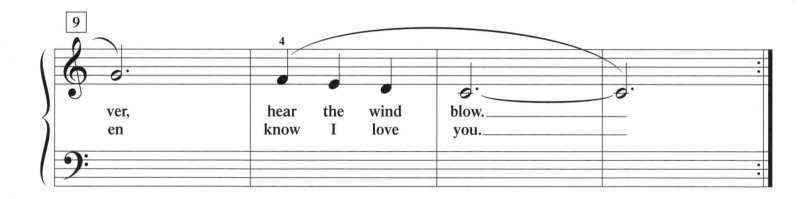

ver,   hear the wind blow._____
en   know I love you._____

Teacher Duet: (Student plays 1 octave higher)

R.H.

L.H. *mp*   *with pedal*

1.   2.   *rit.*

Camptown Races

Middle C Position

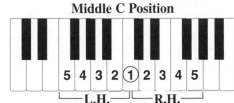

Cheerfully

Camp - town la - dies sing this song, doo - dah, doo - dah;

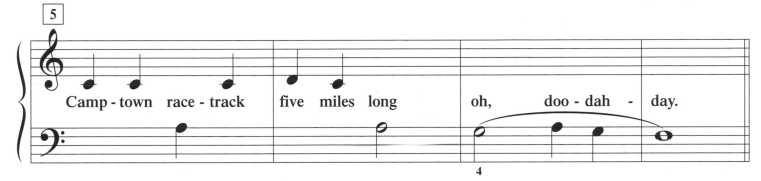

Camp - town race - track five miles long oh, doo - dah - day.

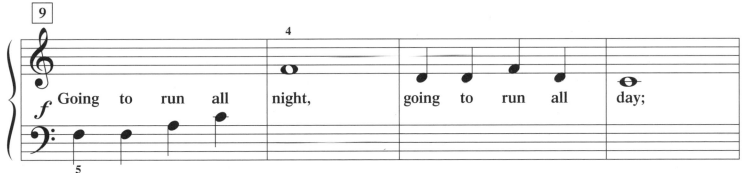

Going to run all night, going to run all day;

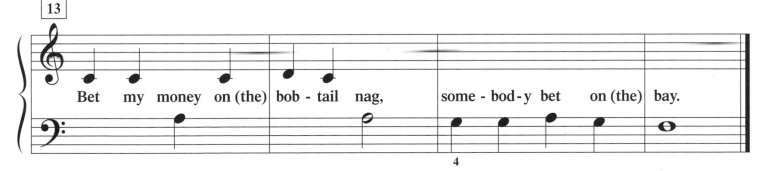

Bet my money on (the) bob - tail nag, some - bod - y bet on (the) bay.

Teacher Duet: (Student plays 1 octave higher)

Middle C Position

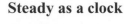

Grandfather's Clock

Henry C. Work

Steady as a clock

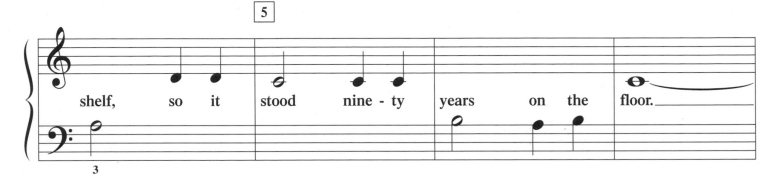

My grand-fa-ther's clock was too large for the

shelf, so it stood nine-ty years on the floor.

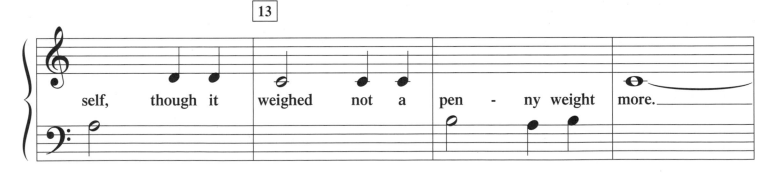

It was tall-er by half than the old man him-

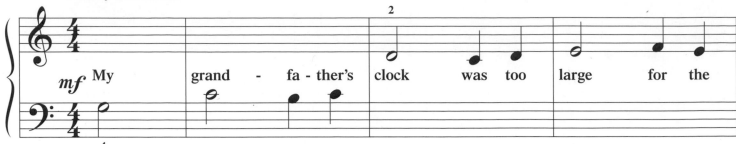

self, though it weighed not a pen - ny weight more.

Teacher Duet: (Student plays 1 octave higher)

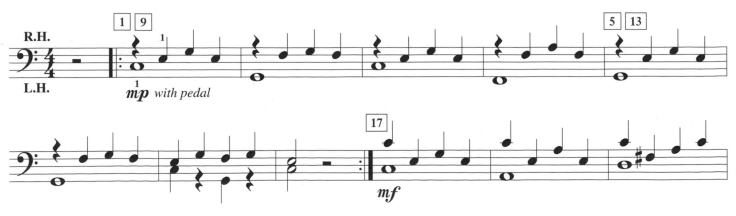

mp with pedal

mf

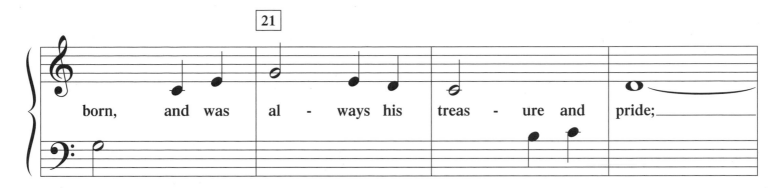

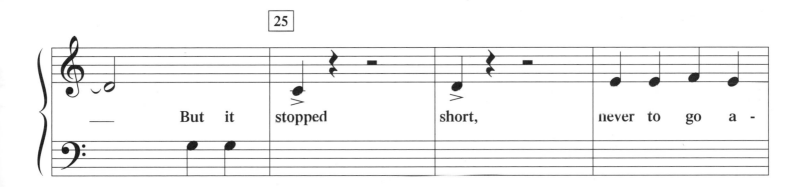

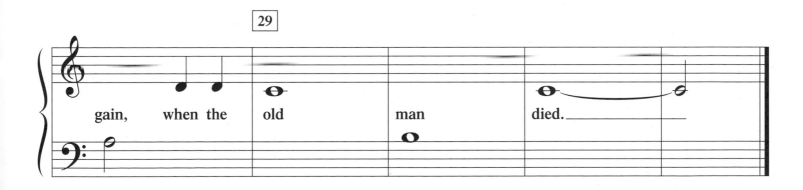

8

Aura Lee

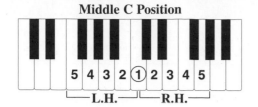
Middle C Position

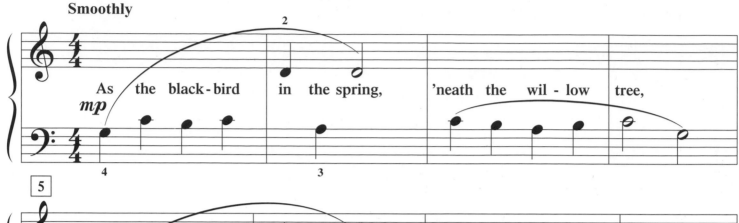

Smoothly

As the black-bird in the spring, 'neath the wil-low tree,

Sat and piped, I heard him sing, sing-ing Au-ra Lee.

Au-ra Lee, Au-ra Lee, maid of gold-en hair,

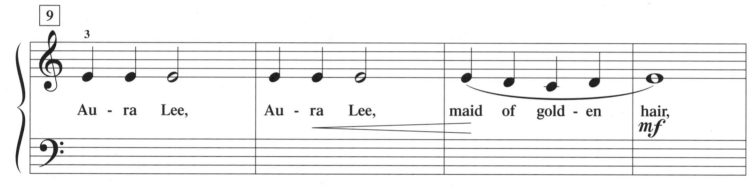

Sun-shine came a-long with thee, and swal-lows in the air.

Teacher Duet: (Student plays 1 octave higher)

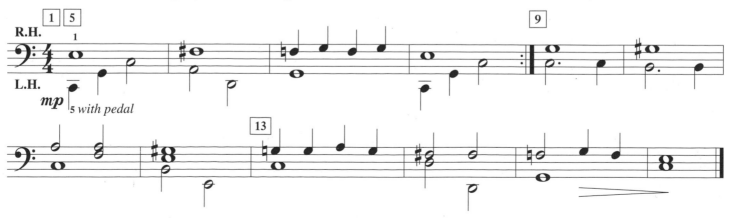

She'll Be Comin' 'Round the Mountain

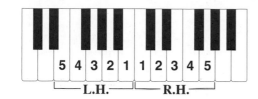

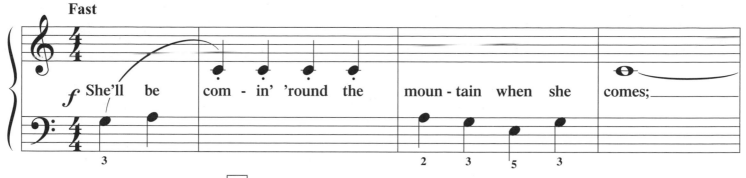

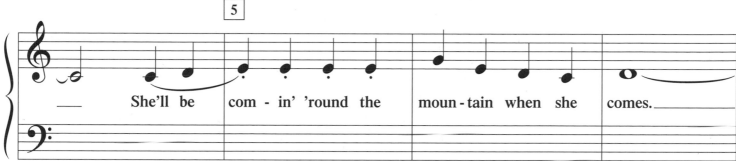

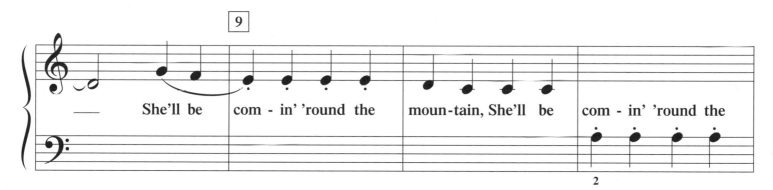

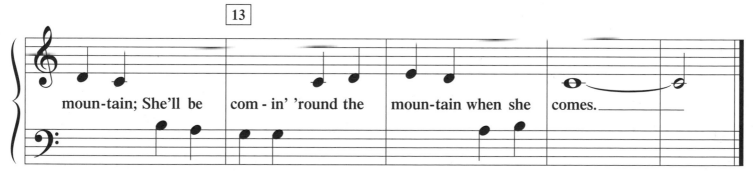

Teacher Duet: (Student plays 1 octave higher)

FF1013

Middle C Position

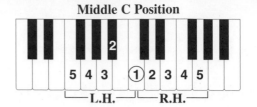

Oh Dear, What Can the Matter Be?

Flowing along

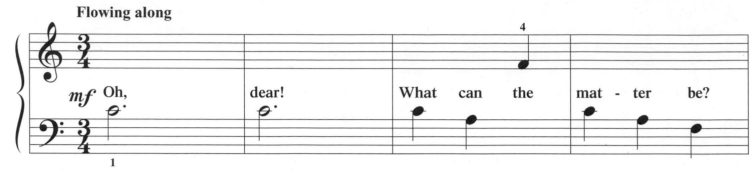

Oh, dear! What can the mat - ter be?

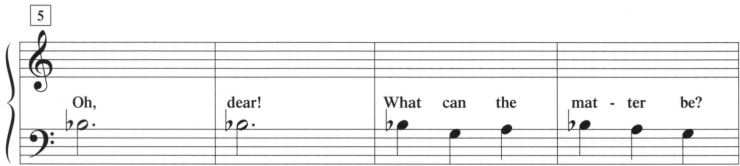

Oh, dear! What can the mat - ter be?

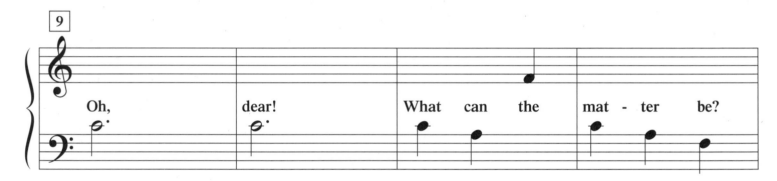

Oh, dear! What can the mat - ter be?

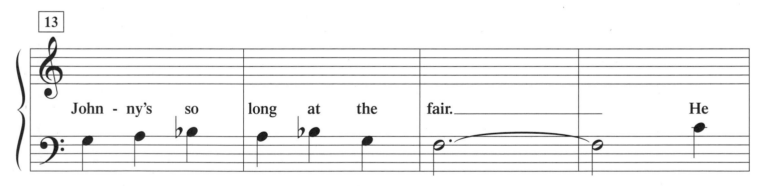

John - ny's so long at the fair._____ He

Teacher Duet: (Student plays 1 octave higher)

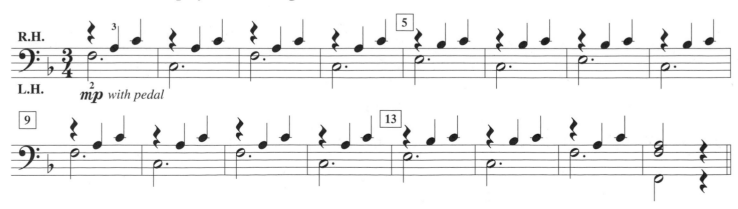

12

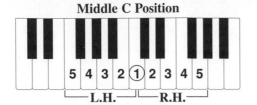

Middle C Position

Oh! Susanna

Stephen C. Foster

With energy

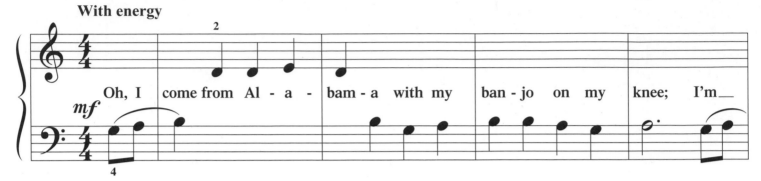

Oh, I | come from Al - a - | bam - a with my | ban - jo on my | knee; I'm___

going to Lou' - si - | an - a my___ | true love for to | see. It___

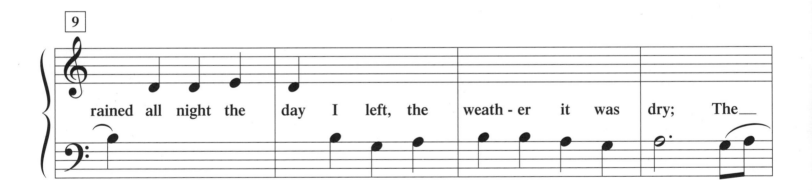

rained all night the | day I left, the | weath - er it was | dry; The___

Teacher Duet: (Student plays 1 octave higher)

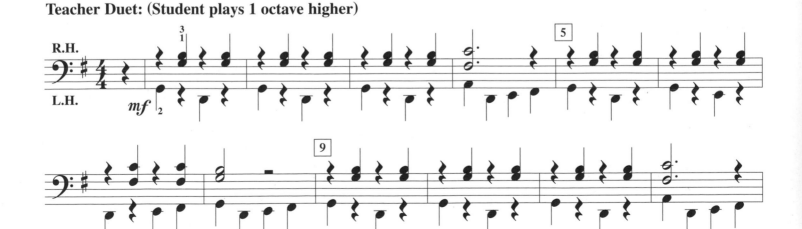

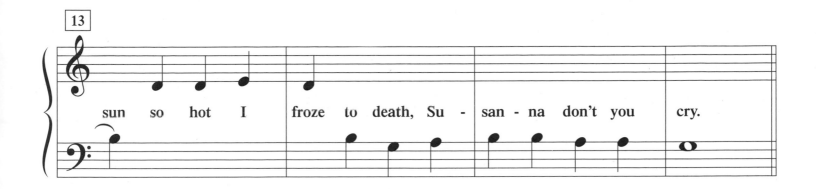

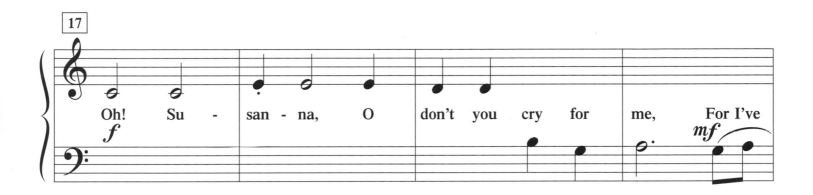

14

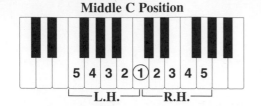

Middle C Position

Home on the Range

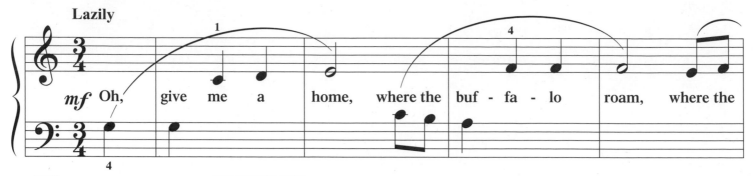

Lazily

mf Oh, give me a home, where the buf - fa - lo roam, where the

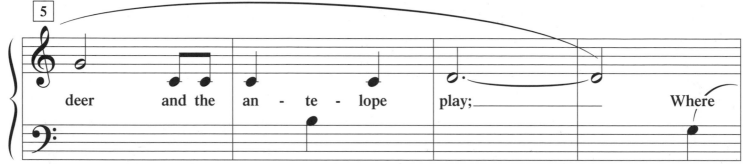

deer and the an - te - lope play;_____ Where

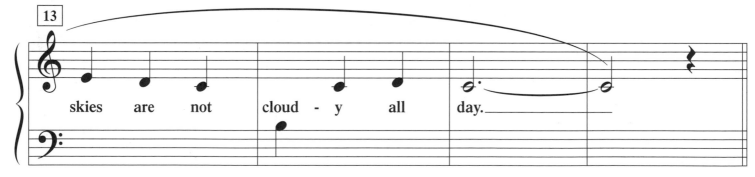

sel - dom is heard a dis - cour - ag - ing word, and the

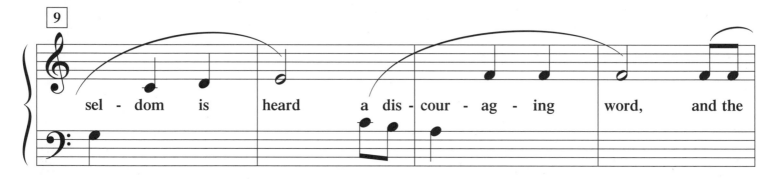

skies are not cloud - y all day._____

Teacher Duet: (Student plays 1 octave higher)

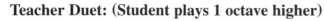

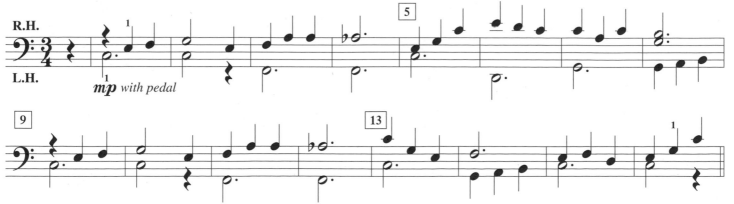

mp with pedal

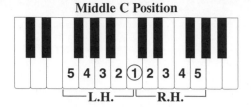

Reveille

U.S. Army Bugle Call

Briskly

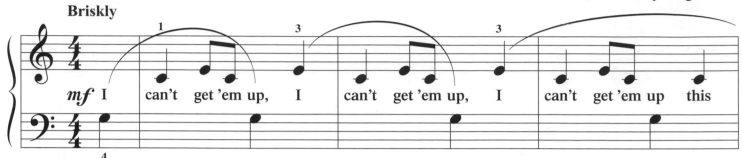

I can't get 'em up, I can't get 'em up, I can't get 'em up this

morn - ing; I can't get 'em up, I can't get 'em up, I can't get 'em up at

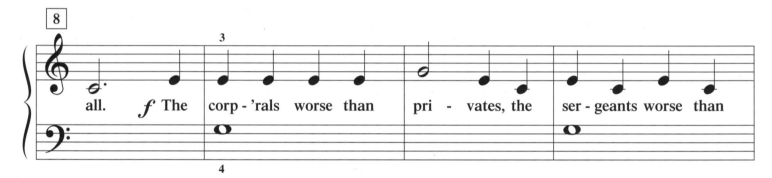

all. *f* The corp - 'rals worse than pri - vates, the ser - geants worse than

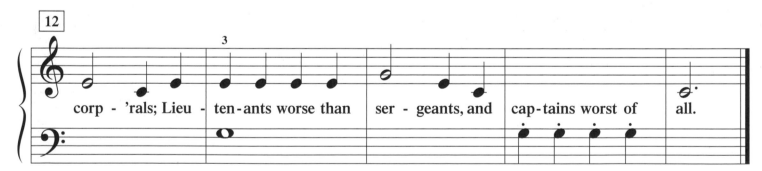

corp - 'rals; Lieu - ten - ants worse than ser - geants, and cap - tains worst of all.

Teacher Duet: (Student plays 1 octave higher)

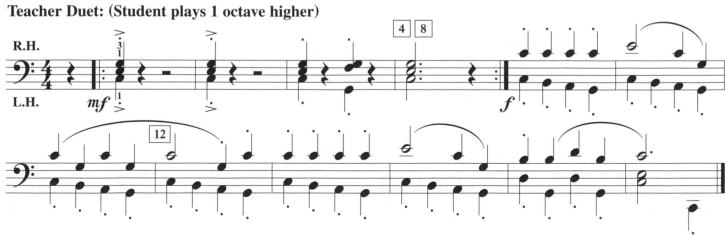

Taps

U.S. Army Bugle Call

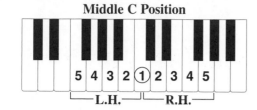

Middle C Position

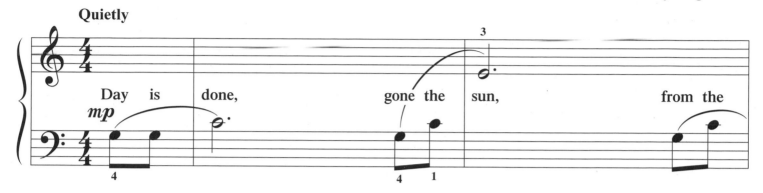

Quietly

mp

Day is done, gone the sun, from the

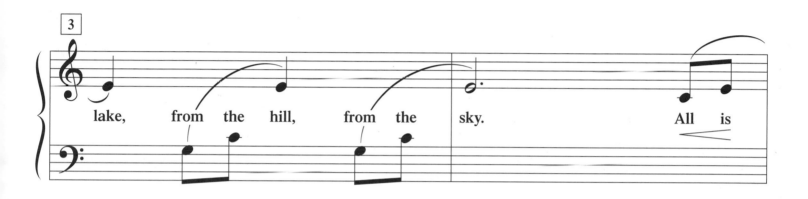

lake, from the hill, from the sky. All is

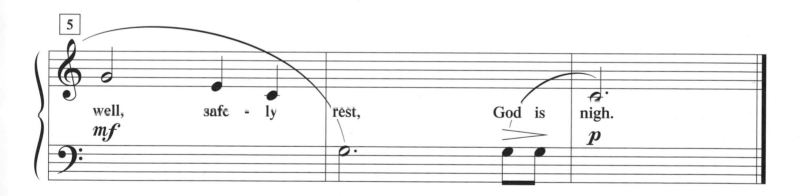

mf

well, safe - ly rest, God is nigh. *p*

Teacher Duet: (Student plays 1 octave higher)

mp

with pedal

FF1012

Middle C Position

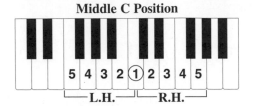

Are You Sleeping

Happily

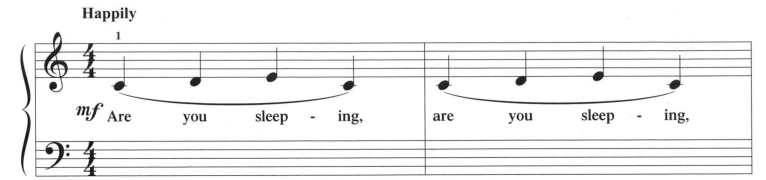

mf Are you sleep - ing, are you sleep - ing,

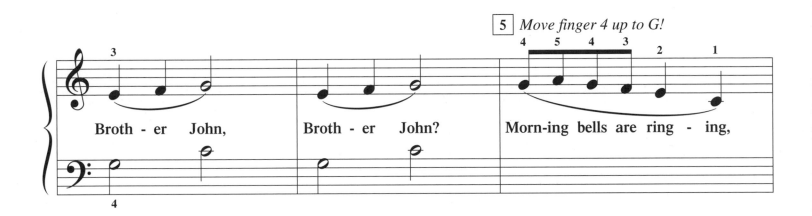

Broth - er John, Broth - er John? **5** *Move finger 4 up to G!* Morn-ing bells are ring - ing,

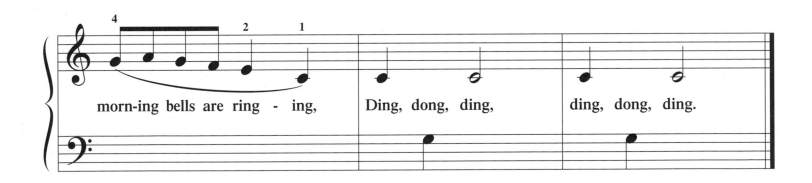

morn-ing bells are ring - ing, Ding, dong, ding, ding, dong, ding.

Teacher Duet: (Student plays 1 octave higher)

R.H.

L.H. mf

Good Night, Ladies!

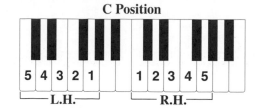

C Position

Merrily

Good - night, la - dies! Good - night, la - dies!

Good - night la - dies, we're going to leave you now.

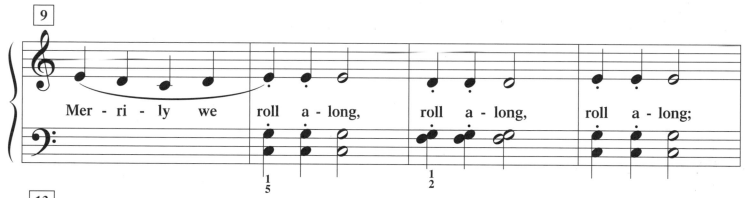

Mer - ri - ly we roll a - long, roll a - long, roll a - long;

Mer - ri - ly we roll a - long, o'er the deep blue sea.

Teacher Duet: (Student plays 1 octave higher)

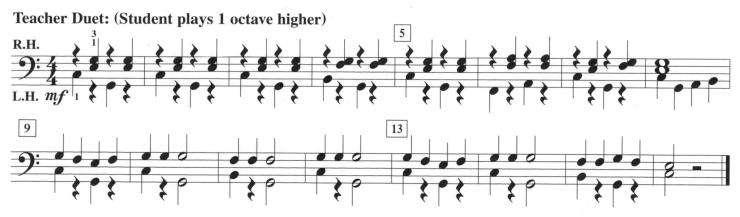

R.H.

L.H.

20

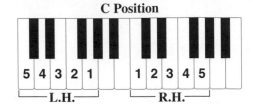

C Position

Sweetly Sings the Donkey

Sweetly

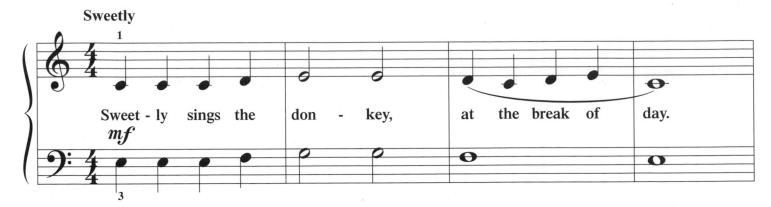

Sweet - ly sings the don - key, at the break of day.

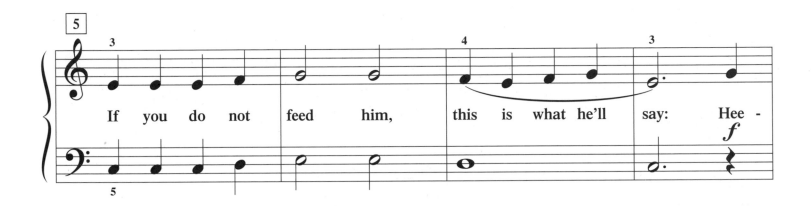

If you do not feed him, this is what he'll say: Hee -

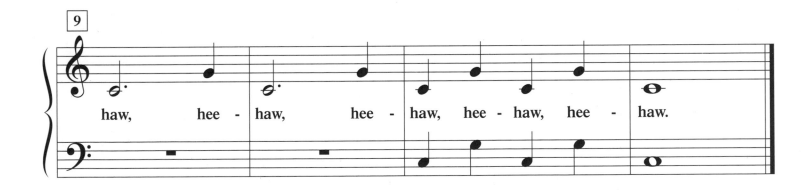

haw, hee - haw, hee - haw, hee - haw, hee - haw.

Teacher Duet: (Student plays 1 octave higher)

When the Saints Go Marching In

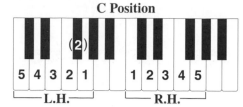

Teacher Duet: (Student plays 1 octave higher)

FF1013

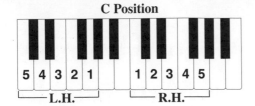

Sleep, Baby Sleep

Peacefully

Sleep, ba - by sleep! It's time to go to sleep. Your

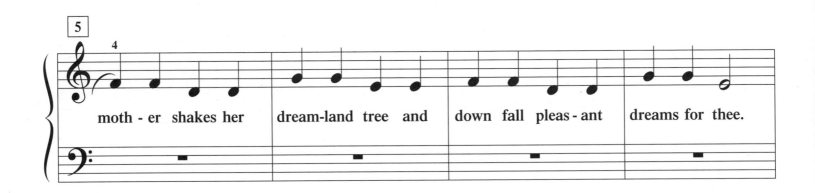

moth - er shakes her dream-land tree and down fall pleas - ant dreams for thee.

Sleep, ba - by sleep. Sleep, ba - by sleep.

Teacher Duet: (Student plays 1 octave higher)

with pedal

C Position

This Old Man

Very steady

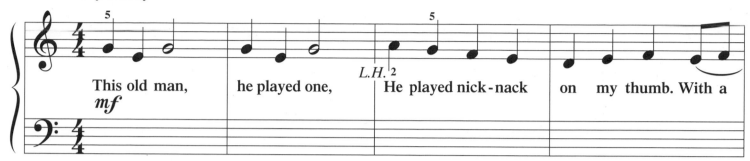

This old man, *mf* he played one, He played nick-nack on my thumb. With a

nick-nack, pad-dy whack, give the dog a bone! This old man came roll-ing home.

2. This old man, he played two,
   He played nick-nack on my shoe.
3. This old man, he played three,
   He played nick-nack on my knee.
4. This old man, he played four,
   He played nick-nack on my door.
5. This old man, he played five,
   He played nick-nack on my hive.
6. This old man, he played six,
   He played nick-nack on my sticks.

7. This old man, he played sev'n,
   He played nick-nack till elev'n.
8. This old man, he played eight,
   He played nick-nack on my gate.
9. This old man, he played nine,
   He played nick-nack on my spine.
10. This old man, he played ten,
    He played nick-nack over again.

Teacher Duet: (Student plays 1 octave higher)

C Position

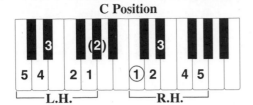

Snake Dance

Mysteriously

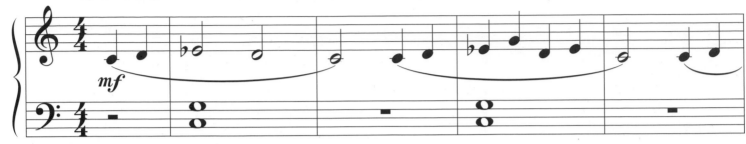

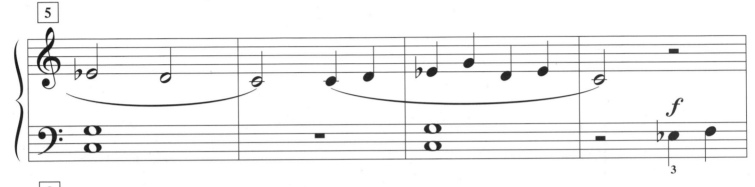

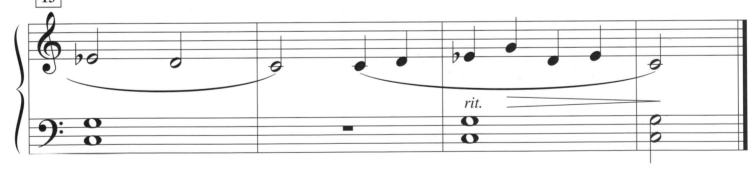

Teacher Duet: (Student plays 1 octave higher)